How To Buy Insurance and Save Money

Visit www.booksurge.com to order additional copies.

How To Buy Insurance and Save Money

D B Heins

HEINS-SITE PUBLISHING

2007

How To Buy Insurance and Save Money

TABLE OF CONTENTS

INTRODUCTION

Let me start by first telling you a little about myself. I started studying insurance when I was a junior in high school. Why? My father was very successful with a major life insurance company and the insurance people I caddied for at the golf club all played well, were nice people, paid me well and took off every Thursday afternoon to play. What I did not know then was they worked longer hours on the other days. I also grew up in the backyard of the largest auto and home insurance company in the United States.

I continued my education by attending and graduating from one of the top insurance colleges in the country with a major in insurance. I have since obtained my CLU® (Chartered Life Underwriter) and CFP® (Certified Financial Planner) designations. I have been an agent, underwriter, claims handler, operations supervisor, agency manager, consultant, and agency executive, and I am now back as a multi line agent. I really doubt anyone has more background in the insurance industry than I do. I really do understand the whole picture.

What I have found is the insurance industry makes insurance difficult to understand, and consequently difficult to buy. Most people don't know what to ask or what to look for when buying insurance. Part of my mission statement as an executive was, and still is, to "make the insurance industry better for consumers." My plan in this book is to simplify insurance and give you the tools and knowledge you need to make good and informed buying decisions. You should save money and better understand the insurance you have, or will buy, after reading this book. I will cover Auto, Home, Life, Health, Long Term Care, and Disability Income insurance coverage. Sound good to you? Then let's do it!

Preface

The counsel you get from an agent is extremely important. A good agent should ask many questions about what is important to you and walk you through each line of coverage. If you have a great agent, you probably don't even need to read this book because he or she should be making sure they design coverage to your particular needs. A good agent might still give you this book just to show you that they are doing a good job. Make sure the agent and staff people are licensed. To be licensed, they have to complete continuing education, and a knowledgeable person is a better resource for you.

Do some research on your insurance company. The company representatives might say they will pay your claims but what does history say about them? Call the local body shops and ask who takes the best care of their customers. It is value you want and the claims-paying part of the package is important. It is also important to do business with a financially secure company. You can find company ratings on line or at your local library. Just ask for Insurance Company Ratings.

Whenever you can, have all of your insurance in one office and with one company. The multi line discounts and other benefits of having all of your insurance in one place are big. Loyalty is also rewarded. Companies will treat you better when you have more lines of coverage with them and have been with them a long time. It is just good business for the company to do so.

Why Insurance?

I know many people who look at insurance as an evil necessity. The reality is without insurance you would not be able to do or buy many of the things you do now. The concept behind insurance is to spread the risk of loss among many so that the consequence of loss to any one is not too great. Think about it. Your bank would not let you buy a home without having insurance unless you have enough cash to cover the loan if the home were destroyed. It is the same with your car. What about a business that did not carry insurance? One mistake or loss and the business may very well have to close. I know not everyone carries life and health insurance. I also know many families who have been saved from financial ruin because they had insurance to offset the cost of death or illness.

Insurance companies invest their money in relatively conservative investments. This means that even when much of the financial world might be in turmoil, insurance companies will be there with money to infuse into the economy. Often it is insurance companies that loan money to banks and other financial institutions, and insurers buy the bonds that help finance many of our infrastructure needs (roads, schools...). Don't let insurance intimidate or scare you. With the help of this book, you will be able to prepare for and understand what you are buying. Always remember that insurance is a financial tool to help you feel more secure.

New Rules for Insurance Rates

If you have not heard of insurance scores, you will. In all lines of insurance, companies are starting to use insurance scores to determine what rate an individual will pay. There are too many variables that go into making up your insurance score to touch on them all, so we will review a few of the big ones that you can control.

Credit Score: I know it is hard to believe, but your credit score is closely correlated to your chances of having a claim.

A good credit score means less chance of a claim. Maybe people with good credit scores just take care of everything they do better than people with poor credit scores. I don't know. Maybe they just pay the little claims themselves. Credit scores can be used to underwrite all types of insurance, including life and health, and it is a very good indicator.

Loss History: If you turn in many claims, your score goes down (bad). With many companies, if you call in and file a claim that ends up not being payable (below your deductible), they still count it in your score. When you call about a claim, make sure they know you do not want to file a claim until they can explain what would happen or what would be paid if you did file one.

Multiple Policies: The more policies you have in one company the better your score with them will be. Although this is also accounted for in the multi line discount companies offer, it may be used in your score too.

Longevity with Carrier: Companies look at how long you have been with them. Longer is better for your score.

There are many factors and combinations that go into making your insurance score. Watching these four will help you keep your score higher, resulting in lower rates.

Auto Insurance

Although states have different laws governing the form of auto insurance written, the basics of what to look for and what to think about are the same. Let's look at the coverage offered by auto insurance.

Liability Coverage: This is coverage for when someone sues you. How much do you need? Well, that depends on how much you have to lose. Picture yourself getting in an accident and it was your fault. The driver of the other car is hurt pretty badly and he or she decides to sue you. The driver's attorney will need to calculate the monetary damage, but will also look at what assets you have. It does no good to sue someone for millions if the person only has $100. On the other hand, if you have a nice home and good bank account, the amount sought could be a big number. At this point, the attorney will probably find out what liability limits the at-fault driver (you) have on your insurance policy. If the limits are high enough, that is probably all the injured person will sue for. My rule of thumb is to have at least enough liability coverage to equal the total value of your assets. You should ask your agent if a liability umbrella is best for you. A liability umbrella provides millions of dollars of protection that go over (on top of) your auto and home insurance. If you have worked your whole life to build a nice nest egg or estate, doesn't it make sense to protect that from being taken due to one mistake?

Medical Coverage: This coverage only pays for medical bills from auto accidents. Most states have a minimum mandatory coverage while others, like Michigan, provide mandatory lifetime benefits for auto injuries. For people who have individual or group health insurance, you need to ask your company how benefits will be paid if you are in an auto accident. If your regular health insurance will pay first (primary coverage) in an auto accident, you can carry less medical coverage under your auto insurance. If they will not pay first, you need to look at each level of coverage and cost, then buy what you feel is the best value for you.

Collision Coverage: This is the coverage that will pay to fix your car when you are in an accident. The premium is often based on the value of the car, or what it would cost to repair it. A choice of deductibles is available. I would advise taking the highest one that allows you to comfortably pay the deductible should you have an accident. Many people used to have a $50 or $100 deductible but we rarely see new policies written with less than a $500 deductible. You might want to set up a side fund at your bank or credit union and put the deductible amount in there. You will also be able to use this concept for your homeowner coverage, so your side fund would work as a self insurance account for both. Do not pay the insurance company to insure something you can self insure.

When people ask, "How old should my car be when I take collision coverage off?" I first ask them what it is worth. You need to look on line or at the library to see what the wholesale value of your car is. Then you can decide pretty easily by comparing the premium you pay for collision coverage per year to what you would get if the car was totaled.

Comprehensive Coverage: This coverage takes care of about any other physical damage to your car, other than a collision. Vandalism, hail storms, a rock into the windshield, theft of the vehicle, hitting a deer...are all comprehensive claims. You will have a separate deductible for this coverage. Again, if you can afford to self insure, you should choose a higher deductible. Comprehensive coverage is usually less expensive than collision coverage, and many people decide to keep comprehensive coverage on a policy even if they drop the collision. Look at the premium and you can decide if it is a good value to you.

Road Service Coverage: This is really convenience coverage. Most people will not go broke paying for a towing bill. Still, it can be good to know you have the coverage should you need it. Some companies require you to use a particular number to call, while others let you choose who to call. Most will pay only up to a specific amount per tow, or to the closest place that can repair your car. Coverage is also provided for getting locked keys out of the car or helping to change a flat tire. If your company does not have an assigned service provider, you will probably have to pay the bill yourself and then be reimbursed by the insurance company. If you have an agent, he or she can often write the reimbursement check from the office directly to you, before you get your credit card bill.

Car Rental: Car rental coverage pays up to a certain amount to help you rent a car while yours is being fixed from a covered loss. When your car is in for routine repair or maintenance, this coverage will not pay. This coverage can be expensive, but the first question most people ask when they call in a claim is, "Do I have car rental coverage?" Think about what you can afford to pay if you don't have the coverage. If it takes 2 weeks to fix your car, and the rental car costs $25 per day, that's over $350. If you have a spare car available, you probably do not need this coverage.

Uninsured/Underinsured Motorist: Ok, now let's say you are in an accident and hurt badly. This time the other driver is at fault and you decide to sue him or her. You find out the other driver does not have many assets and does not have high enough limits on his or her liability coverage to cover your damages. Uninsured/Underinsured coverage allows you to come back against your own insurance policy to collect up to whatever limits you have selected. My advice is to carry the same limits here as you do for your liability limits. Give yourself as much coverage as you have provided for if someone were to sue you.

Death Indemnity: Many people look at this as life insurance; however, it is very limited protection. The death or injury has to have been caused by an auto accident. If you buy this coverage, it should not be counted as part of your life insurance program. You should not make your family's well being dependent on your being killed in an auto accident.

Other optional coverage: There are new policies and coverage coming on the market all the time. If you feel one of them are important, go for it. Just remember they all cost money and the insurance company does not plan on losing money on any of them. That's not bad; they are businesses. Just don't buy coverage you really don't need. Maybe you can invest your savings for retirement!

Liability and Auto Insurance Worksheet

This is used to determine how much liability coverage you need. How much are you worth? Home(s) $_____
Cars $_____ Toys $_____
Savings $_____ Other $_____
         Total $_____
Carry at least as much liability coverage dollars as you have dollars in assets, up to 5 million dollars. You may do this with an Umbrella policy. At a minimum people should consider $100,000 of liability coverage regardless of assets.

Auto information needed

1. Driver's license numbers of all household drivers

2. Vehicle Identification Numbers of all vehicles

3. How far each of the cars are driven weekly, and for what purpose (pleasure, work, school...?)

4. How much of your savings is readily at hand (easy to get quickly)? Write this number down and think about how much of that you can use for a self insurance account $_____

5. What is the value of your car(s) if sold wholesale? This information should be used to decide if you want to carry collision coverage. Look this up on line or at the library:
    $_____ $_____ $_____ $_____

6. Does your health insurance carrier pay first (primary coverage) you if you are injured in an auto accident?

HOMEOWNER/ RENTER/CONDO OWNER INSURANCE

Your lender will require you to carry Homeowners insurance, and it makes sense to insure one of your biggest, if not the biggest, physical assets. Coverage is pretty straight forward if you know what to look for.

Building: What if your house burned down? Would your coverage be enough to rebuild it? This is not what the house would sell for, but what it would take to build the same house at today's prices. Most insurance companies have computer programs that will give a very good estimate on what it takes to rebuild your home but the final decision is always up to you. Insurance companies will usually give you extra coverage, if you insure it for what they think it should be insured for. They do this because building materials and labor can fluctuate (such as after a hurricane) so you need the coverage to expand in case that happens. Your coverage probably contains an inflation rider that will automatically help your insurance keep pace with the rising cost of building or repairing your home.

Other Structures: This will be 10% of your building coverage, unless you pay for it to be more. It covers any buildings on the property that are not attached to the home. If you have put up a nice outbuilding or have more than one unattached structure, you need to confirm that you have enough "other structures" coverage.

Personal Property: Personal property includes your clothes, TV/stereo, furniture, toys, and just about everything that would not be part of the building. How much do you need? Insurance companies automatically give homeowners between 60 and 75% (varies by company) of whatever the building is insured for to cover personal items. Ask if you can have replacement cost coverage. It is a good idea to take pictures of your personal property and keep them off-site. If you have a claim, your first responsibility is to make an inventory of what was lost, and having pictures makes that a lot easier. A video is best, and easiest.

Loss of Use: If your home burns down or there is so much smoke damage from a smaller fire that you need to be put up somewhere, this coverage pays for a hotel room, condo, rental house...until you can get back into your home. It also gives some money for the extra cost of eating out. Most companies give you a specific dollar amount for coverage. Others say they will pay whatever that actual cost is. Often companies limit this coverage to one year, and that can be a problem. In many cases, the chances of you getting the old home taken down and a new one built all within a year are small. Be sure to stay on top of the claims and building process. If your company gives you two years of benefits under this coverage, you should be fine.

Medical payments: This is liability coverage designed to take care of people who get injured while at your home. Say a friend comes over and slips on the stairs, requiring stitches. Even if he has medical coverage, he might seek damages to cover the deductible. This coverage will pay for that. Insurance companies would rather pay under this coverage and handle it quickly because it lessens the risk of being sued for more. The limits under this coverage are usually $1,000. This coverage does not cover resident family members or someone working at your home.

Liability: Here we have the same situation as with Auto insurance. You need to have enough so that if sued the person suing will not go after your assets. The umbrella policy discussed in the Auto section could also provide coverage here.

Damage to property of others: This is like a little liability coverage for property damage you or a household family member might cause. A great example is when my nine-year- old son was sure he could hit a golf ball over the neighbor's house, but only got it as high as the first floor window. Covered!

Back up of sewer and drain: Although this sounds like great coverage to have, it is very limited in what it covers and it usually carries a separate large deductible. It's easy to understand why really, because only people who think they will need it buy it, right? It might be good to have this coverage but be sure you understand what is covered and what the limits are.

Personal Articles Coverage: Some companies sell this as a separate policy, while some offer it as a rider. It provides coverage for more types of losses than the regular homeowner contract. For example, if my niece came over and jumped on my 12 string guitar, my homeowner's policy would not cover that. A personal article policy does. This coverage is for the special things you own like jewelry, collections, cameras...Many of these items often have limited coverage under a standard homeowner's policy. Be sure to ask what limits your homeowner's policy has.

Condo Unit Owner: Condominium polices are very similar to a homeowner's policy. First, be sure you understand what the bylaws of your association say you must cover. Some say you must cover any improvements to your building (finished basement, new fireplace, upgraded cabinets...). You might also ask what the condominium association policy covers. Personal property is often the toughest thing to guess, but err on the high side because guessing a little high will not cost much more in premium.

Renter: Renters often think the building owner insures their personal belongings in case of a fire. Not true! Renters, listen up; you need a renters policy to cover your belongings. And don't think your landlord's policy will cover you if someone is injured in your apartment. The landlord's policy will exclude it, so you better have liability coverage! A renter's policy will provide the personal property and liability coverage you need. By the time you get the multi-line discount on your car insurance, adding a renters policy will probably cost close to nothing.

The other coverage under a homeowner's, condo unit owner's or renter's policy is standard and you usually do not have the option to increase or decrease the amounts. Ask your agent what other options you might have.

HOMEOWNER/ RENTER/CONDO OWNER WORKSHEET

1. How much do you think it would cost to rebuild your home if it burned to the ground? Your insurance company agents will tell you what they think but remember the final number is up to you. $_____

2. How much personal property do you have in your home/ apartment? Renters and Condo owners will need to know this to get a quote. Homeowners need to have an idea so they can verify the coverage included in their policy is sufficient. $_____

3. Do you have special collections or jewelry that you want individual coverage on? If so you will need appraisals on each collection or item.

4. If the value of buildings not attached to your home is greater than 10% of the amount your home is insured for, how much more would you need to rebuild those buildings in a total loss (tornado)? $_____ (Total of all out buildings) —minus $_____ (10% of the amount your home is insured for) = equals $_____, and this is how much additional other structures coverage you need.

5. Is replacement cost coverage available from the insurance company?

6. What is the premium savings for going to the next higher deductible?

Life Insurance

The life insurance industry seems to complicate this coverage. It is a shame, too, because it can be simple. Unlike auto and home insurance, life insurance is rarely required by the government or a bank. It is your choice to buy life insurance if you feel you have an obligation that might last longer than your life. I have read that you need 5 to 7 times your annual income. If you want to be a little more specific, get out a sheet of paper and draw a line down the middle (for two people). Now, answer the following questions for each person:

1. How much will it cost to be buried and pay final expenses such as medical bills? Most people plan on between 8 and 15 thousand dollars.   *_____
                                                                                   *_____

2. How much is your mortgage?   *_____

3. Are there other debts to pay off? If so, what is
   the total?   *_____

4. For each person whose income is used to pay
   household expenses, what is the income?   A_____ B_____

5. It is recommended you have 70% of what was coming in before a breadwinner's death, assuming the mortgage, other debts, and a college fund are taken care of. Total the number in #4 and multiply by 70%. $_____

6. For each person who has income higher than the answer to #5, what is the difference? (#4-#5)   A_____ B_____

7. Now multiply the answer in #6 by the number of years you want to have income of the deceased person replaced.   *_____

8. Do you want to provide funds for a college education for your children? If yes, how much total for all?   *_____

9. Now total these five numbers   *=_____

10. What is the total of your current life insurance
    and savings?   _____

11. #9 minus #10 is a good estimate of what
    you need. $ _____

Some people may want to deduct what social security would pay to the survivors from the annual income needs. Just remember Social Security pays a dependent child until he/she is 18 (up to age 19 if attending elementary or secondary school full time), and only pays the surviving spouse until your youngest child is 16. The benefits might change as the belt tightens on Social Security so be sure to check on line at http://www.ssa.gov/.

If you have a sizable estate, you will want to work with an attorney/planner to look for ways to lower and pay the probable estate taxes. One more note, after you determine the insurance needed, figure out what you can afford to pay in premium to cover that need. Can you afford a dollar a day or two, three, four, five..., or annually a specific amount? Be honest with yourself. If you can buy all you need with that budgeted amount, great! If you can't, buy what you can. The purpose of life insurance is not to make you feel broke; it should relieve pressure rather than create it.

Types of Life Insurance

There are many names for different life insurance policies, but they all come down to term and permanent or a mix of the two. Which is better depends on what you are trying to accomplish. When you hear someone say only one or the other is good, it means the person really doesn't understand the whole picture. Also, if you hear someone refer to Life Insurance as a good investment, be very careful. Life insurance might be part of an overall investment plan, but you must first need life insurance. I have both term and permanent and nobody understands it better than I do.

Term Life Insurance:

The easiest way to think about term insurance is to compare it to renting or leasing a home. You get the use of the home for whatever the length of the lease and the cost per year is set for the lease period. The cost might go up during the lease (term) so be sure to ask. At the end of the lease you can renew it (up to a certain age), but the cost will have gone up. And as you approach 60, 70, 75 years of age, the cost will probably be prohibitive. So you will have either died and the benefit was paid to your beneficiary, or you out lived the coverage and walk away. No equity, no value, but you did have the coverage for the time you were paying. Remember this; term life insurance in the younger and mid years costs much less than permanent life insurance. But just like when you get to the end of renting a home and need to move on, you will have no equity.

Permanent Life Insurance

Buying permanent life insurance is like buying a home in that the cost will be higher initially but the payment remains the same. And you will build equity, just like you do in a home.

Should you decide to take some of that equity out, it will be a loan against the face value of the policy, just like a home equity loan is against the value of the home. Equity in the permanent policy does not build quickly early on, unless you have a hybrid that allows you to put more money into it sooner. These hybrids are being watched closely by the IRS so be aware before you buy one. When tax benefits promised during the sale sound too good to be true, they probably are.

So which is better for you?? Term does cost less in the beginning when most people need more (young kids, big mortgage). As you start to earn more and have the dollars available, consider converting some of that to permanent life insurance. You may have heard "buy term and invest the difference." When someone says, 'I'll do term and invest," I say, "Great idea." Then a few years later I ask how the savings are going. Rarely does the person have much saved. The "savings" have been spent for new cars or new washers or new furniture, or...whatever. You see, savings only works if it compounds. Permanent insurance does help you to force yourself to save and leave the money alone. Next, if you need the coverage for 20 years or more, you will probably have to average 4% to 5% return on the savings between the cost of term and permanent to break even with what the value is in the permanent policy. Now I know people can earn higher rates than this. I advise people to have a mixed portfolio with some aggressive, some moderate, and some conservative investments. For the conservative part of the portfolio, permanent life insurance is great. Even if you end up cashing the policy in at retirement, you have the option of taking the payments as an annuity, and the payout rates in some policies are still very good. With permanent coverage, you can take some cash out when you retire; leaving enough to pay the premiums and provide the amount of death benefit you want. Could you do much the same with buying bonds? I think so, but then you don't have options when you get older and still want or need some life insurance.

Why do I have both term and permanent life insurance? I recently purchased a lake home and I wanted to cover the mortgage. I don't plan on needing it a long time, so term makes the best sense. And I have to tell you that when 9/11 and the tech stock slides hit the market, it was great to know my permanent life insurance was still going up in value at the same rate it had been before. I could count on it. I even used some of the cash values to buy real estate at an opportune time. Both term and permanent provide me value to meet specific goals and needs that I have.

Remember to decide what your budget allows you to spend on life insurance. Don't buy something you feel bad about paying for, OK?

HEALTH INSURANCE

Our health insurance system used to be the best. It is not now. A few years back I was certain the government needed to get out of the health insurance business. Ever since it got involved, the prices started going crazy. The reality is government needs to be involved to the extent that it promotes competition. The consumer has not really cared about what the bill from the doctor or hospital was because the consumer only paid the deductible anyway, right? Our economy is based on market place competition keeping prices down, and that competition does not exist in our health care. Health Savings Accounts (HSA) are currently gaining momentum. They are a good way to promote competition. My fear is they will not grow fast enough to stop the demand for getting coverage for everyone, regardless of the effect on competition. That would result in prices actually going up, or quality going down or both. As of the writing of this book, to be an eligible individual and qualify for an HSA, you must meet the following requirements.

- You have a high deductible health plan (HDHP) which has a higher annual deductible than typical health plans. A HDHP also must have a maximum limit on the sum of the annual deductible and out-of-pocket medical expenses that you must pay for covered expenses. Out-of-pocket expenses include co-payments and other amounts, but do not include premiums.
- You have no other major health coverage.
- You are not enrolled in Medicare.
- You cannot be claimed as a dependent on someone else's tax return.

If you meet these requirements, you are an eligible individual even if your spouse has non-HDHP family coverage, provided your spouse's coverage does not cover you. Be sure to check current IRS requirements for HSA eligibility.

If you are eligible to have a HSA, look closely at it. In nearly every case I have run for people, they will win taking the HSA. How does it work? Individuals and families can qualify for an HSA by purchasing health coverage with a large deductible. Let's say you choose a $5,000 deductible with 100% coverage after that. Odds are this will save you a bunch on the premiums you pay. Take those savings and put them into a HSA. Your contributions into the HSA are tax deductible just like contributions to an IRA or 401K plan. You can use the money in the HSA to pay for medical expenses that are not paid under your health plan. For our family, we saved $4,000 in premiums so it almost entirely funded the $5,000 HSA. Last year we had only $2,000 in expenses that we needed to pay for with the HSA money, leaving us $3,000 to start the next year with. If I want, I can put the entire allowable contribution in again each year so my savings account would really start to grow! So how does this promote competition? That $2,000 we spent was not wasted. We made sure we were getting the best service for price for those health expenses. We did so because the money was ours, not the insurance company's or the government's. Health insurance can often equal or surpass what you pay for a car or house payment on an annual basis. Think what would happen if we all watched medical expenses the same way we did when looking for value in a new car or home. I have included a HSA worksheet at my web site (dbheins.com) for you to review. Put in the numbers and see if it works for you.

What if you are not eligible to have a HSA? The same principle of taking the highest deductible you can afford applies. Like all insurance, you pay more for lower deductibles than they are worth because from the insurance company standpoint, lower deductible claims have many of the same costs as higher deductible claims (paper work, computer time, and so on). Almost all plans have some deductible you pay first, and then you and the insurance company share the cost (coinsurance) at a specific rate. The company might pay 80% while you pay 20%. There is also usually a stop-loss or maximum out-of-pocket limit for you each year. This maximum will be for each individual insured, or for all insured family members, or both. The last common factor in health insurance is the lifetime or annual maximum the insurance company will pay. I have seen this as small as $250,000 and as big as unlimited, although most are between 1 and 8 million dollars for lifetime now. I wouldn't go for anything less than 1 million, but be sure to check the cost and determine the best value for you.

HMO, PPO or Traditional Health plans: HMOs have gotten

a bad rap. They are a way to limit health care cost by limiting your choices to within a network. Doctors and hospitals in that network have agreed to charge a lesser amount for many procedures. The care you get within the network is probably just as good as you get from anywhere. The problem is people feel trapped in HMOs, and if that is the case, even a lower price might not entice them to join.

The traditional health insurance plans let you choose whatever doctor or care facility you want. Along with this freedom of choice comes the most expensive premium. Many times I have seen traditional plans cost double what a HMO plan cost.

The PPO (Preferred Provider Organization) is a mix of the other two. You can go to any doctor or facility you want, but if you go to one outside of the PPO you will have to pay additional deductibles or coinsurance rates.

A benefit some plans are offering is wellness care. They pay for you to have a physical every couple of years. These physicals help reduce future claims by identifying potential problems (high blood pressure, cholesterol, diabetes…). Some even offer discounts at local health clubs. What a great idea! Lower health cost by lowering the chances of problems. If these benefits are available, be sure to take advantage of them.

Health Insurance Worksheet

1. Do you qualify for having a HSA? Your group insurance representative or agent will know.

2. What plans are available? PPO, HMO, Traditional?

3. What are the deductibles?

4. What are the coinsurance rates?

5. What is the lifetime or annual maximum benefit?

6. What is the stop-loss or out-of-pocket maximum per person and/or family?

7. How are prescription drugs handled?

8. Are there any wellness benefits?

9. How are pre-existing conditions handled?

Long Term Care Insurance

This is a new coverage, when compared to the others we have reviewed. Its purpose is to provide money and/or options when someone needs long term care. Options might include care in the home, day care facility, training for the caregiver, and all the way to care in a facility on a full time basis. There are many companies selling Long Term Care (LTC) products but most have the same options. Currently, people who have limited income and assets have long term care paid by Medicaid. Medicaid is not Medicare. Medicare provides almost no benefits for long term care. Medicaid is a program run by each individual state to help provide care for low income people. I am not sure how long states can or will continue to pay for long term care because it's a huge part of the budget. What else can they do? I don't know, but there is only so much money available and at some point they will have to decide who gets benefits and who does not. I do know it will only get tougher to qualify for Medicaid to pay for long term care.

Daily Benefit: You will want to find out the daily rate charged by local facilities by calling a couple of the long term care facilities in your area to ask what the current daily rates are. I would then consider buying about 80-90% of the average. Why not 100%? Most people in these facilities are on Social Security and will continue to receive those payments. Use your Social Security and or pension income to offset the remaining 10-20%.

Length of Benefit: You can choose from 1 year all the way up to lifetime (no limit), but the cost goes up greatly for extending the benefit length. The average stay is about 2½ years, so use this information along with what your budget allows to pick your benefit.

Elimination period: Most companies offer from 30 day to 180 day elimination periods. Do you have some money in the bank or income that could help pay for the first few months of care? If you do, then choose the longer elimination periods and your premium will be less.

Inflation Rider: This coverage increases your daily benefit by a certain percentage each year. It can either be a compound increase or a simple increase. The compound increase costs more because the benefit increase is based on the prior year benefit. A simple increase will always increase the benefit by the percentage of the original daily benefit. I like the simple benefit because I believe competition will help keep prices in check for long term care, so the simple benefit increase should be sufficient. The simple increase benefit also costs much less.

With the four options listed so far, you can have great flexibility in price. Play around with different coverage and find the one that makes best sense to you.

On the Long Term Care question sheet, I will include questions related to other features and benefits you should ask about. Many states require a form to be completed that helps individuals determine if Long Term Care insurance is appropriate for them, so ask your agent about this. There may also be tax advantages to having Long Term Care insurance and your agent or accountant should be able to describe them to you.

Long Term Care Worksheet

1. What is the average daily cost of being in a long term care facility in your area? $ _____

2. Do you have savings that could be used to offset the cost for a few months? If so, what is the appropriate elimination period for you?

3. What benefit is there for Home Health Care?

4. What benefit is there for care at a day care center?

5. Is there a benefit for Home Modification so that you can receive care in your current house rather than going to a facility?

6. What are the requirements to be eligible for benefits? Usually there is a list of daily activities a person can no longer perform (bathing, eating, toileting, dressing, transferring, continence), or if the person needs supervision due to severe cognitive impairment.

7. Is there a bed reservation benefit? You need this in case a person has to leave the facility (to go to the hospital for care) and then come back to the LTC facility.

8. What type of inflation guard is there, and what is the cost?

9. Is there a safety clause in case a premium payment is missed?

10. Is there a spousal discount?

DISABILITY INCOME

Disability income coverage is one of the most neglected types of insurance. The reality is you have a much better chance of becoming disabled than you do of dying. And without your income replaced, you will likely lose everything if you suffer a long term disability. Many people think Social Security will pay them but, in fact, most disability claims for Social Security are denied, and if you do receive benefits, it is not usually until 18 or more months of being disabled. Good disability coverage can be expensive, especially if you're in an occupation that is considered a higher risk class. So what do you do to cover yourself?

First, put aside money into that self insurance fund we talked about early in this book. Six months of income in savings will allow you to take a much longer elimination period for disability insurance, and this greatly reduces the premium. Next, understand that you can only buy up to about 70% replacement of income for a benefit because in most cases the benefit will be income tax free. You will have the option of buying a benefit that pays for 1 year or longer, up to a benefit that pays to age 65. Your budget will be your guide. Other things to look at are your employer's benefits and asking if they have long term (more than 180 days) disability coverage available. You will probably want to take it if they do. You might also find lower price products that will cover loans and can be purchased through the lender. The lender might not always have the best premiums, so check around. The benefits for these loan based products usually only provide a 3 to 5 year benefit, but that might be all you can afford so go with it. Even 3 to 5 years of benefits if you are disabled will allow you and your family to breathe a little easier while figuring out what to do.

Some disability policies have an "Own Occupation" definition versus "Any Occupation." Own occupation means you will be considered disabled if you can not perform the duties of the job you had prior to disability. Any occupation says you are disabled only if you can not be trained to do some type of work. There are limits and further definitions associated with both of these so be sure to ask what the definition of disability is. Own occupation definition policies will cost more.

Another way of reducing premium cost is to find a policy that has benefits that will be reduced by what ever income you earn or Social Security benefits you receive. For instance, if you are receiving a full benefit of $2,000 per month and then qualify for $1,000 in Social Security benefits, your benefit under your policy will drop by $1,000.

Disability Income Worksheet

1. How much is your savings and how long will that keep you paying your bills if you became disabled? Use this information to determine an elimination period.

2. If you are an employee, you will need to prove how much money you make. Your most recent pay stub will do.

3. If you are self employed, you will be required to present your last year tax return.

4. Ask your employer what disability benefits are available for you.

5. What is the definition of disability in the policies you are considering?

6. What benefit period works best for your budget?

THE FUTURE OF INSURANCE

(I HOPE)

I'd really like to see things simplified. Rather than having to buy liability coverage under your home insurance and car insurance and boat insurance and........ Just have one policy that covers everything. Same with physical damage coverage whether it is for your home, car, boat........ How can this be done? Simple, if we get (not just think) outside of the box.

You should be able to walk in, call in, or click in to an insurance company and tell the agent what cars you have, the value of rebuilding your home, the amount of liability coverage you need, and how much you can afford out of pocket in case of a loss. You also could tell the agent what your mortgage is, your current income, your other debts, and what cash needs you know you will have in the near future (10-20 years). With this information, the agent could write one policy to cover all your physical property and liability risk and one to cover premature death or disability. You would have the same deductible if something happened to your car or if your house burned down. In areas that require very high deductibles for catastrophic risk (hurricanes, brush fires...), those could be taken care of with one paragraph explaining this.

Next, allow people to have tax deductible Insurance Savings Accounts (ISA). In these plans people would save money without being taxed on the earnings. The money could be taken out to cover deductibles for covered losses. As your savings account grows, you could increase your deductible which would lower your premium and give you additional savings. It would be like the HSA rules for health insurance, but applied to all types of individual insurance.

As an incentive to low income families, they could use some of the funds to do regularly required upkeep of their homes (new roof, new siding, upgrade electrical wiring are a few examples). I would even recommend matching contributions from the government for low income families to help them establish these accounts. As people feel more secure and can save more, their property will go up in value increasing not only pride of ownership but also increasing the tax base of their community. We give big business tax breaks; let's give some incentive to the low income people.

These are just a couple of ideas on how to make insurance consumer friendly. We would need some form of national standards or rules over insurance and financial services for them to be implemented. In the big picture, they both make a ton of sense because they are good for the customer and promote competition. If these ideas are implemented, twenty years from now people will be saving more and they will better understand what their insurance does for them. Would you agree that saving money and better understanding will lead to better value? There you go!

Thanks for reading, and if anyone asks who told you about the ideas in this book, please tell them "D.B. Heins." Peace to all, Doug

www.ingramcontent.com/pod-product-compliance
Lightning Source LLC
Chambersburg PA
CBHW051258170526
45165CB00004B/1769